·THE·WORLD·OF·
ATLANTA

Created by Norman Shavin
Photography by Chipp Jamison

Published by
Capricorn Corporation, Inc., • 4961 Rebel Trail, NW • Atlanta, Georgia 30327 (USA)
United States of America

Acknowledgements

In the development of this book, three individuals deserve primary credit for contributing their intense dedication, creative skills and energies. They are superior, and without them I would not have undertaken a project of such magnitude.

Norman Bloom, of Norman Bloom Enterprises, was involved in the project from inception, and performed as an invaluable associate in the development of the book, its marketing and promotion. My appreciation of his skill, good humor under trying circumstances, and his passion for this project is boundless.

Chipp Jamison's photographs speak for themselves. He is obviously a splendid craftsman, an artist who demands of himself the best.

Kathy King, who designed the book and made significant contributions to its overall concept, has worked with me before, and for good reason: She functions remarkably under pressure and treats each project as a personal statement of value. She is a prize.

Without them all this book would not have been possible.

NORMAN SHAVIN

"The World of Atlanta" is published and distributed by Capricorn Corp., Inc., 4961 Rebel Trail, NW, Atlanta, Georgia 30327 (United States of America). Phone: (404) 843-8668. [An illustrated list of its titles will be sent on receipt of a self-addressed, stamped envelope.]

Copyright © 1983 and 1986 to "The World of Atlanta" is held by Capricorn Corp., Inc., and Norman Bloom Enterprises, to which all rights are reserved, except for the photographs, which are Copyright © 1983 and 1986 by Chipp Jamison, to whom photographic copyright is reserved.

"The World of Atlanta" was produced in association with Norman Bloom Enterprises.

Second Edition: ISBN 0-910719-18-7.

Book design by Kathleen Oldenburg King.

Mechanicals by Olio 2 Advertising.

Typesetting by The Scotch Type Shop, Inc., and the Japanese Linguistic Service.

Translations by the Inlingua School of Languages and the Japanese Linguistic Service.

Printing by Phoenix Communications, Inc.

Binding by National Library Bindery.

For signed, limited edition color prints of any of the photographs, contact Chipp Jamison, Earthwork Studio, 2131 Liddell Drive, NE, Atlanta, Georgia 30324. Phone: (404) 873-3636.

The pages of this book reflect a very special place. If you want to know more about any aspect of it, contact:

Les pages de ce livre reflètent un lieu unique. Si vous voulez en apprendre plus sur un de ses aspects, contactez:

Die Seiten dieses Buches strahlt einen besonderen Platz zurücck. Sollten Sie mehr darüber erfahren wollen, wenden Sie sich an:

Las páginas de este libro reflejan un lugar muy particular. Si Usted quiere saber más sobre cualquiera de sus aspectos, contacte:

本紙はアトランタでも特に大切な場所を紹介しています。
詳細をお求めの方は下記までご照会ください。

Roy B. Cooper
Atlanta Chamber of Commerce
P.O. Box 1740
Atlanta, Ga. 30301 (USA)
Phone: (404) 521-0845

MAYOR ANDREW YOUNG
City of Atlanta

As former U. S. Ambassador to the United Nations I learned how small the world is, and how similar all people are in their hopes and dreams. As mayor of Georgia's largest city I continue to work in behalf of international understanding.

Atlanta, 150 years old, is a vibrant capital of opportunity, a city of tremendous appeal for all the world.

Like this exciting book, Atlanta opens its doors to all people who wish to call it home, and who bring to it the desire to make Atlanta even greater through their talent and labor.

MAYOR

Lorsque j'étais Ambassadeur des Etats-Unis aux Nations Unies, j'ai rémarqué que le monde était petit et que tous les peuples ont les mêmes rêves et les mêmes espoirs. En tant que maire de la plus grande ville de Georgie, je m'efforce toujours de contribuer à la compréhension entre les nations.

La ville d'Atlanta, qui a 150 ans, est une ville en pleine croissance qui présente beaucoup d'attraits pour les hommes et les femmes du monde entier.

Ce livre montre qu'Atlanta ouvre ses portes à tous ceux qui veulent y vivre et l'enrichir par leur talent et leur ardeur.

LE MAIRE

Als früherer Botschafter der USA bei den Vereinten Nationen habe ich gelernt, wie klein die Welt ist und wie ähnlich sich die Menschen in ihren Träumen und Hoffnungen sind. Als Bürgermeister der größten Stadt Georgias setze ich meine Bemühungen für internationale Verständigung fort.

Die 150 Jahre alte Stadt Atlanta ist ein pulsierendes Geschäftszentrum, eine Stadt mit einem ungeheuren Anziehungsvermögen für alle Welt.

Wie dieses erregende Buch, öffnet Atlanta seine Tore allen denjenigen, die es Zuhause nennen wollen und die mit dem Wunsch kommen, Atlanta durch ihre Arbeit und ihre Begabung noch größer zu machen.

BÜRGERMEISTER

Como anterior Embajador de los Estados Unidos ante las Naciones Unidas aprendí lo pequeño que es el mundo, y lo similar que es toda la gente en sus sueños y esperanzas. Como Alcalde de la ciudad más grande del Estado de Georgia continúo mi labor en bien de la comprensión internacional.

Atlanta, con 150 años de antigüedad, es una vibrante capital de oportunidades, una ciudad con una tremenda atracción para todo el mundo.

Al igual que este excitante libro, Atlanta abre sus puertas a toda la gente que desee llamarle hogar, y que trae consigo el deseo de hacer una Atlanta más grande todavía mediante su trabajo y talento.

ALCALDE

私は米国国連大使としての職務を通じ、世界がいかに小さなものであるか、また全世界の人々がいずれも同様の夢と希望を持っていることを知りました。

アトランタは１５０年前に設立され、現在では活気に満ちた機会の地として世界中の注目を集めています。

本書からも御理解頂けるとおり、アトランタはより偉大な都市を築くべく技能と活力を持って当地を訪れる人々を心から歓迎申し上げます。

GOV. JOE FRANK HARRIS
State of Georgia

For more than 250 years, since Georgia was first settled as a colony, our state has developed a warm tradition of welcoming those who bring their vision, energy and creativity to this land of opportunity.

International trade leads to international friendship, and world peace is served by both.

This book, "The World of Atlanta," illustrates this city at its best, and represents the hospitality that all Georgians extend to those who have come to help us build our land into a great civilization.

GOVERNOR

Depuis l'établissement de la Colonie de Georgie il y a 250 ans, cet état a toujours accueilli ceux qui lui apportaient leur esprit, leur énergie, et leur créativité.

Le commerce international favorise l'amitié entre les peuples, et donc la paix dans le monde.

"Le Monde d'Atlanta" montre cette ville sous son plus beau jour, et représente l'hospitalité dont tous les Georgiens témoignent à ceux qui sont venus construire avec eux.

LE GOUVERNEUR

Seit Georgia vor mehr als 250 Jahren zum ersten Mal besiedelt wurde, hat der Staat eine schöne Tradition entwickelt, alle Menschen willkommen zu heißen, die ihre Energie, ihre Schöpfungskraft und ihr Vorstellungsvermögen in dieses Land der unbegrenzten Möglichkeiten bringen.

Internationale Handelsbeziehungen führen zu internationaler Freundschaft – und beides dient dem Weltfrieden.

Das Buch "Die Welt Atlantas" zeigt die Stadt von ihrer besten Seite. Es stellt die Gastfreundschaft dar, welche die Bewohner Georgias denjenigen bezeugen, die zum Aufbau einer großen Kulturgesellschaft in unserem Lande beitragen.

GOUVERNEUR

Por más de 250 años, desde que Georgia fue establecida como colonia, nuestro Estado ha desarrollado uns cordial tradición de brazos abiertos hacia todos aquellos que traen consigo su visión, energía y creatividad a esta tierra de oportunidades.

El comercio internacional conlleva a la amistad internacional, y la paz mundial se sirve de ambos.

Este libro, "El Mundo de Atlanta", muestra lo mejor de esta ciudad, y representa la hospitalidad que todos los habitantes de Georgia extienden a aquellos que han venido a ayudarnos a convertir nuestra tierra en una gran civilización.

GOBERNADOR

ジョージア州は当地への入植が開始されて以来２５０年以上にわたり新天地をめざすビジョンと活力そして創造力にあふれる人々を暖かく迎えて来ました。

国際貿易は国際友好、ひいては世界的平和につながります。

本書「ワールド　オブ　アランタ」はこの都市の特長を描くと共に、偉大な文明の建設に貢献すべくこの地を訪れる人々に対するジョージア州民の歓迎の意を示すものであります。

Foreword

"The World of Atlanta" was created as a bouquet to the city and its people. Its focus is to illustrate some elements representative of Atlanta at its best and most colorful by depicting how and where area residents work, live and play.

Confirming Atlanta's thrust as an international center, "The World of Atlanta" is the first such book offering data in five languages.

By an easy-to-follow arrangement of headlines and captions in English, French, German, Spanish and Japanese – consistently in that order – "The World of Atlanta" appeals not only to the resident and others interested in Atlanta, but also reaches out to the increasing number of persons visiting from abroad. Indeed, copies of "The World of Atlanta" are being distributed abroad.

The photo captions are purposely spare, and the translations capture the English data sometimes literally, sometimes with allowances for nuances and idioms peculiar to other languages. We hope the translations will encourage readers to develop some understanding of languages other than their native tongues, an ambition easier accomplished when reading familiar alphabetical symbols. Japanese symbols are relatively unfamiliar to Caucasians, but inclusion of that language is justified by the increasing interest of Japanese nationals in this area.

In some cases, readers will find that English proper names are left intact in translated forms; that is the appropriate style. In rare cases where only English and Japanese captions appear, the reader is right to assume that the French, German and Spanish versions are identical to the English.

Dedication

Although Atlanta is a relatively young city by comparison with some historic European and Oriental places, it has been peopled by visionaries and achievers since before its incorporation in 1847. From humble beginnings as a railroad terminus, metropolitan Atlanta has become an energetic area of some 2 million people. Its growth as a transportation, financial, educational, convention and medical center has been remarkable.

Its residents have survived war, military occupation, devastating fire and debilitating economic depression. From each painful setback, Atlantans have been fired with renewed zeal to make of their city a special place.

They have carved it from a forest, but live in balance with its natural beauty; they have harnessed initiative to dreams, and sculptured magnificent structures of commerce; they have sought tranquillity of living, and crafted imaginative homes.

To those Atlantans – past and present – who have showered their talents on this area, this book is dedicated. And to those Atlantans unborn, perhaps "The World of Atlanta" will stimulate their continuance of the area's saga of creativity.

In a personal vein, the author and photographer dedicate this book also to their families: to Phyllis Shavin, the author's wife, and their children – Julie, Mark and Dana...

And to Judy Jamison, the photographer's wife, and their sons, Chase and Ian.

Welcome to the world of Atlanta...

Bienvenue à l'univers d'Atlanta
Willkommen in Atlantas Welt...
Bienvenidos al mundo de Atlanta...
アトランタの町にようこそ・・・

Hartsfield Atlanta International Airport
Hartsfield, l'aéroport international d'Atlanta
Hartsfield Atlanta, Internationaler Flughafen
Hartsfield, el aeropuento internacional de Atlanta
ハーツフィールド・アトランタ国際空港到着

...a city of splendid architecture...

...une ville à l'architecture splendide...
...eine Stadt mit herrlicher Architektur...
...una ciudad de espléndida arquitectura...
・・・みごとな建造物の立ち並ぶ町・・・

Georgia-Pacific Building
L'immeuble de Georgia-Pacific
Georgia-Pacific Bau
El edificio Georgia-Pacific
ジョージア・パシフィック・ビル

...people with hearts...

...aux habitants accueillants...
...Menschen mit Herz...
...gente cordial...
・・・豊かな心・・・

. . . carefree restaurants . . .

. . .aux restaurants décontractés. . .
. . .angenehmen Restaurants. . .
. . .simpáticos restaurantes. . .
・・・ゆったりとしたレストラン・・・

Michelle's (Georgia-Pacific Building)
Michelle's (L'Immeuble de Georgia-Pacific)
Michelle's (Georgia-Pacific Bau)
Michelle's (El edificio Georgia-Pacific)
ミッシェルズ（ジョージア・パシフィック・ビル内レストラン）

...fantastic technology...

...à la technologie de pointe...
...phantastischer Technik...
...tecnología de avanzada...
・・・すばらしいテクノロジー・・・

...and year 'round recreation.

...offrant des divertissements toute l'année.
...und ganzjähriger Erholung.
...y diversiones durante todo el año.
・・・四季を通じて楽しめるレクリエーション。

Solar research: Georgia Tech
La recherche sur l'énergie solaire: Georgia Tech
Sonnenenergieforschung der Georgia Technischen Hochschule
Investigación en energía solar: Georgia Tech
太陽エネルギーの研究: ジョージア・テク

On the Chattachoochee
Sur la Chattahoochee
Am Chattachoocheefluss
El río Chattachoochee
チャタフーチー河で

There is diversity in Atlanta's nature...

La nature d'Atlanta est très diversifiée...
Es gibt Mannigfaltigkeit in Atlantas Charakteristik...
Atlanta le ofrece variedad en sus paisajes...
アトランタの自然は色とりどり・・・

...and in its homes.

...et ses demeures aussi.
...und in privaten Wohnstätten.
...y en sus viviendas.
・・・そして住宅も千差万別。

It is a city for worshipping...

C'est une ville pour la prière...
Es ist eine Stadt um zu beten...
Es una ciudad para rezar...
崇拝の町・・・

Cathedral of Christ the King
Kathedrale "Christus der König"
La cathédrale du Christ Roi
Catedral de Cristo Rey
キリスト・ザ・キング大寺院

. . . and working . . .

...et le travail...
...und arbeiten...
...y trabajar...
・・・勤勉の町・・・

. . .le théâtre. . .
. . .sich am Schauspiel zu erfreuen. . .
. . .ir al teatro. . .
・・・レジャーをエンジョイし・・・

. . .et le jeu.
. . .und an Spielen Spass zu haben.
. . .y disfrutar de la vida.
・・・エンジョイするために遊ぶ町。

Alliance Theatre
アライアンス（連合）劇場

Atlanta: a world of surprises.

Atlanta: un monde plein de surprises.
Atlanta, eine Welt der Ueberraschungen.
Atlanta: un mundo de sorpresas.
アトランタはハプニングがいっぱい。

A dramatic kitchen
Une cuisine spectaculaire
Eine dramatische Küche
Una cocina espectacular
演出満々のコックさん

You can run the Peachtree Road Race...

Vous pouves participer à la course de Peachtree Road...
Sie können in der Peachtree Road Race mitlaufen...
Usted puede participar en el maratón Peachtree Road...
ピーチツリー街レースに参加したり・・・

The race begins...
La course commence...
Das Wettrennen fängt an...
Largada de la maratón..
競技は始まり…

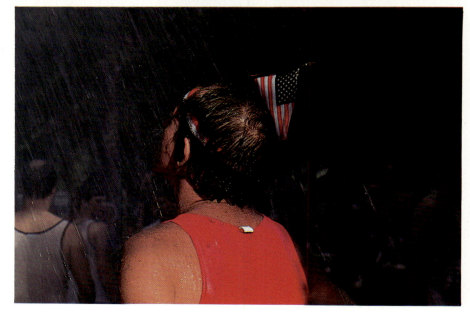

. . .and ends.
. . .et finit.
. . .und hört auf.
. . .su llegada.
…そして終る。

Next page: The handicapped compete, too.
Page suivante: Les handicapés y participent aussi.
Nächste Seite: Die Benachteiligten machen auch mit.
Página siguiente: Los lisiados también participan.
次ページ：身体障害者も競技に参加。

...or sit for baseball.

...ou suivre un match de baseball.

...order einem Baseballspiel zusehen.

...o asistir a un partido de béisbol.

・・・それとも、腰かけて野球の見物。

Revel in its beauty from afar...

Réjouissez-vous de sa beauté à distance...
Für ihre Schönheit von ferne schwärmen...
Deléitese con su belleza a la distancia...
美は遠くから・・・

. . . or up close . . .

. . .ou de près . . .
. . .oder in der Nähe . . .
. . .o de más cerca . . .
・・・それとも、もっと近づいて・・・

Sculpture on Peachtree
Sculpture sur Peachtree
Skulptur an der Peachtreestrasse
Escultura en Peachtree
ピーチツリーの彫刻

Element of Firemen's Fund Building
Une vue de l'immeuble Firemen's Fund
Bestandteil des Firemen's Fund Bau
Un área del edificio Firemen's Fund
ファイアーマンズ・ファンド・ビルの一角

. . . from the outside . . .

. . . de l'extérieur . . .
. . . von draussen . . .
. . . desde sus exteriores . . .
・・・外から・・・

Georgia-Pacific Building in the clouds; fountain at Piedmont Center
L'immeuble de Georgia-Pacific dans les nuages; une fontaine à Piedmont Center
Georgia-Pacific Bau in den Wolken; Springbrunnen am Piedmont Zentrum
El edificio Georgia-Pacific entre las nubes; fuente en el Piedmont Center
雲にかかったジョージア・パシフィック・ビル; ピードモント・センターの噴水

. . .to the inside. . .
. . .à l'intérieur. . .
. . .nach Innen. . .
. . .e interiores. . .
• • •内まで• • •

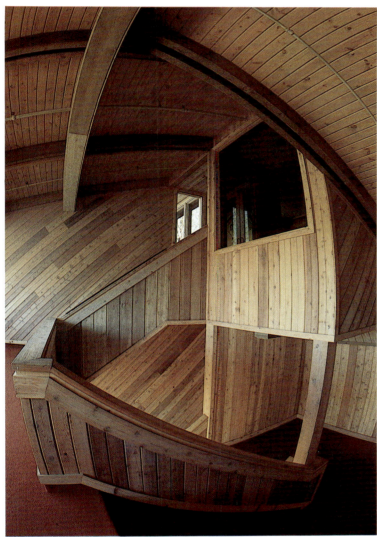 

Office building interiors; right, inside the Hurt
A l'intérieur d'immeubles commerciaux; à droite: dans l'immeuble Hurt
Bürohaus Inneneinrichtung; rechts, in dem "Hurt"
Interiores del edificio de oficinas; a la derecha, interior del edificio Hurt
オフィスビルのインテリア: 右はハートビル内部

. . . and in the faces.

...et sur ses visages.
...und in den Mienen.
...hasta en los rostros.
・・・そして、一人一人の顔にも。

Whatever your pleasure, from ballet...

...to a parade...

Quoi que vous aimiez, la danse classique...

Was immer Ihr Vergnügen ist, vom Atlanta Ballet...

Chalesquiera sean sus gustos, desde un ballet...

レジャーなら、もうおまかせ。バレーから・・・

...ou un défilé...

...zu einer Parade...

...hasta un desfile...

・・・パレードにいたるまで・・・

The Atlanta Ballet
L'Atlanta Ballet
Das Atlanta Ballet
El Atlanta Ballet
アトランタ・バレー

The Fourth of July Parade
Le défilé du 4 juillét
Die Vierte Juli-Parade
El desfile del 4 de Julio
独立記念日のパレード

. . . Atlanta appeals to every mood.

...Atlanta peut satisfaire tous les goûts.
...Atlanta reizt zu jeder Stimmung.
...Atlanta los satisface todos.
・・・アトランタは、どんなムードにもぴったり。

Limelight Entertainment Complex
Le Limelight: une boîte de nuit animée
Limelight Unterhaltungszentrum
Limelight, un night-club imponente
演芸催し物施設

Concert in Robert W. Woodruff Park
Un concert à Robert W. Woodruff Park
Konzert im Robert W. Woodruff Park
Concierto en el Robert W. Woodruff Park
セントラル・シティ・パークでのコンサート

Next Page: Six Flags Great American Scream Machine
Page suivante: Les impressionnantes montagnes russes du Parc d'attractions de Six Flags
Nachste Seite: Six Flags' "Grosse amerikanische Schreimachine"
Página siguiente: La espeluznante montaña rusa de Six Flags
次ページ：シックス・フラッグのグレート・アメリカン・スクリーム・マシン

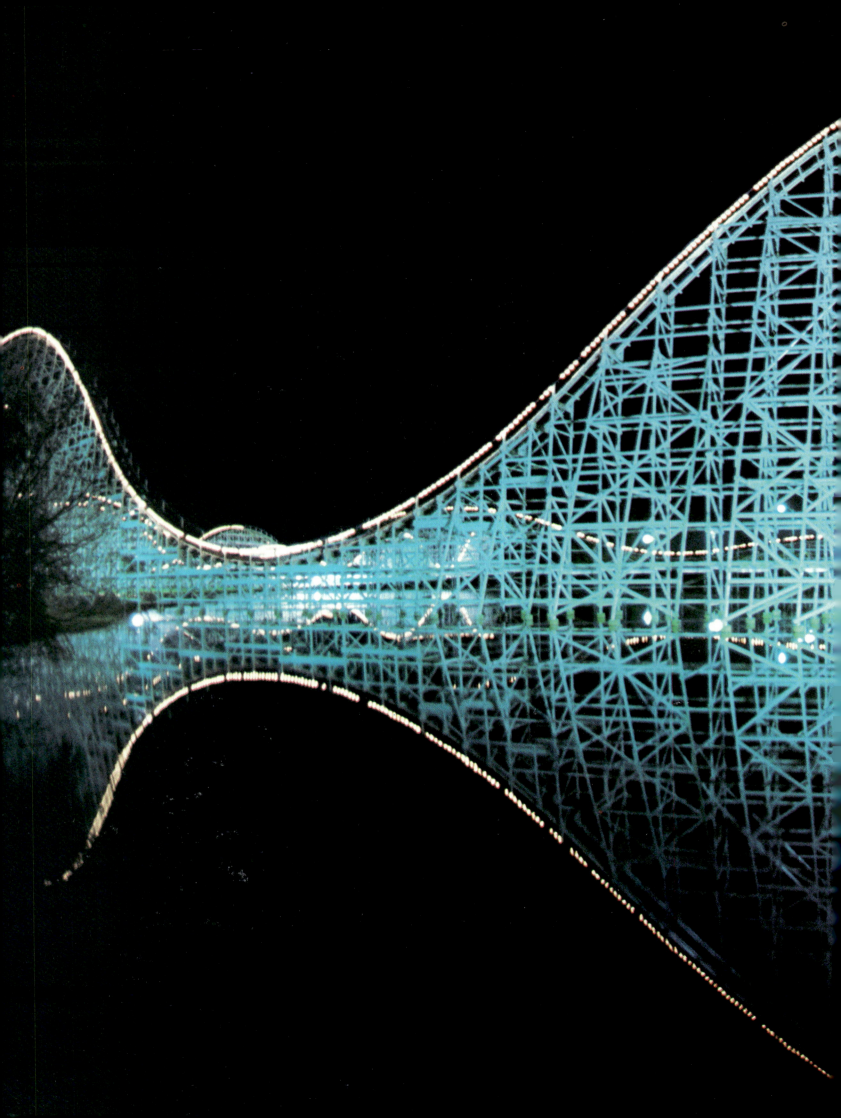

It is an historic treasure to contemplate...

C'est un trésor historique que l'on peut contempler...
Sie ist als geschichtlicher Schatz zu betrachten...
Es un patrimonio histórico para contemplar...
昔を思い・。・

Oakland Cemetery
Le crimetière d'Oakland
Oakland Friedhof
Cemeterio Oakland
オークランド墓地

U.S. Cemetery, Marietta
Le cimetière U.S. de Marietta
U.S. Soldatenfriedhof, Marietta
Cementerio de los E.E.U.U., Marietta
マリエッタの合衆国墓地

Tomb of Dr. Martin Luther King Jr. at Center for Non-violent Social Change
La tombe du Docteur Martin Luther King, Jr. au Centre pour le Changement Social par la Non-violence
Grabstätte von Dr. Martin King, Jr. im Zentrum für gewaltlosen sozialen Wechsel
Tumba del Dr. Martin Luther King, Jr. en el Centro para Cambios Sociales No-violentos
非暴力社会改革センターにあるマーチン・ルーサー・キング・ジュニア博士の墓石

. . .to remember the past. . .

. . .pour se souvenir du passé. . .
. . .sich der Vergangenheit zu erinnern. . .
. . .para recordar el pasado. . .
・・・昔をしのぶに・・・

. . .and celebrate the present.

. . .et célébrer le présent.
. . .und die Gegenwart zu feiern.
. . .y celebrar el presente.
・・・そして、現在を祝福するに・・・ここに歴史の宝庫がある。

Battle of Atlanta Cyclorama at Grant Park
Le cyclorama de la Bataille d'Atlanta à Grant Park
Schlacht von Atlanta im Cyclorama, Grant Park
Ciclorama de la Batalla de Atlanta, en Grant Park
アトランタの合戦を描いたグランド・パークの円形パノラマ

"Light-Up Atlanta" Celebration downtown
Le festival "Light-Up Atlanta" dans le centre de la ville
"Beleuchte Atlanta" Festlichkeiten in der Innenstadt
Festival "Light-Up Atlanta", en el centro de la ciudad
"アトランタに灯を"の祭典、ダウンタウンで

The rapid transit system: a moving experience...

Le réseau de transports publics: un grand dynamisme...
Das Untergrundbahasystem: eine rollende Ehrfahrung...
El dinámico servicio de transportes: gran mobilidad...
高速輸送システム: 走る・・・

MARTA train leaving Martin Luther King Jr. Center Station
Une rame de MARTA quitte la station Martin Luther King Jr. Center
MARTA Untergrundbahn verlässt Martin Luther King Jr. Center Station
Un tren del servicio MARTA sale de la estación Martin Luther King Jr. Center
ファイブ・ポイント・ステーションを発車するマルタ電車

...between stations...through the earth.

...entre les stations...et sous terre.
...zwischen Stationen...unterirdisch.
...entre estaciones...horadando la tierra.
・・・駅から駅へと・・・地球をかける。

Rapid transit stations
Quelques stations de métro
S-Bahnhöfe
Estaciones del transporte rápido
高速電車の駅

Next Page: Digging the MARTA subway
Page suivante: Le métro MARTA en cours de construction
Nächste Seite: Ausgrabungen für die MARTA Untergrundbahn
La siguiente página: El subterráneo MARTA en construcción
次ページ: マルタ地下鉄土木工事

From exquisite homes...

Des résidences élégantes...
Von ausserordentlich schönen Häusern...
Desde elegantísimas casas...
エレガントな住宅から・・・

. . .to exciting shopping. . .

. . .au shopping passionnant. . .
. . .zu interessanten Läden. . .
. . .hasta las compras más entusiasmantes. . .
・・・愉快なショッピングにいたるまで・・・

Lenox Square
Lenox Square
Lenox Square
Lenox Square
レノックス・スクエア

Rich's at Lenox
Le grand magasin Rich's à Lenox
Rich's Warehaus in Lenox
Las grandes tiendas Rich's en Lenox
レノックス街のリッチズ・デパート

. . . from the unusual . . .

. . . de l'insolite . . .
. . . vom Ungewöhnlichen . . .
. . . desde lo inusual . . .
・・・珍しい品あり・・・

Small stuffed dolls . . . and big body-builders on display
De petites poupées de chiffon . . . et un concours de culturisme
Kleine ausgestopfte Puppen . . . und Starke Männer mit riesigen Muskeln sind ausgestellt
Pequeñas muñecas de trap . . . y exhibición de musculatura
ちっちゃなぬいぐるみ……たくましい筋肉が自慢の男達

...to the sublime...

...au sublime...
...zum Erhabenen...
...hasta lo más sublime...
・・・貴重な品ありで・・・

Atlanta Symphony in Memorial Arts Center
L'orchestre Symphonique d'Atlanta au Memorial Arts Center
Atlanta Sinfonie im Memorial Kunst Zentrum
Orquesta Sinfónica de Atlanta en el Memorial Arts Center
メモリアル・アート・センター（記念美術会館）でのアトランタ・シンフォニー

...Atlantans cherish beauty, fun...

...les habitants d'Atlanta aiment la beauté, les rires...
...Atlantaner hegen und pflegen Schönheit, lieben Spass...
...los habitantes de Atlanta valoran la belleza, la diversión...
・・・アトランタは美と喜びの世界をいつくしみ・・・

Clowns at "Light-Up Atlanta" celebration
Des clowns au festival "Light-Up Atlanta"
Clowns bei der "Light-Up Atlanta" Feier
Payasos en la celebración "Light-Up Atlanta"
" アトランタに灯を" の祭典でおどけてみせるピエロ

. . . work . . . and enterprise.

. . . le travail . . . et l'esprit d'initiative.
. . . Arbeit . . . und Geschäftsunternehmung.
. . . el trabajo . . . y la iniciativa.
・・・仕事と・・・実業の機会を提供する。

Shopping can be down-to-earth...

Le shopping peut être un retour à la nature...
Einkaufen kann erdgebunden sein...
Ir de compras puede ser algo sencillo, como antaño...
ショッピングは現実的に・・・

Farmers' markets
Le Marché
Farmer's Markt
Ferias y Mercados Alimenticios
野菜の市、ファーマーズ・マーケット

...and a galactic laser show explosive.

...ou le spectacle éblouissant et galactique des rayons laser.

...und sternartige, aufregende Laser Vorführung.

...o explosivo como un show galáctico de rayos laser.

・・・空には銀河のレーザー・ショーがほとばしる。

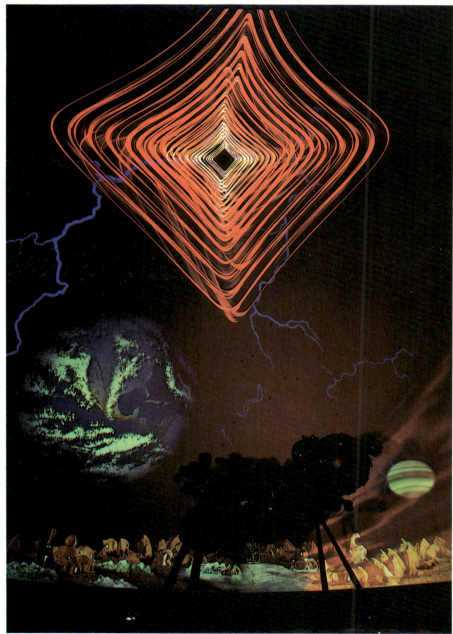

Laser show at Fernbank Science Center Planetarium (also next page)
Le spectacle de rayons laser au Planétarium du Fernbank Science Center (page suivante également)
Laser Vorfhrung von dem Planetarium Fernbank Wissenschaftszentrum (auch nachste Seite)
Show de rayos laser en el Planetario del Centro Fernbank Science (también la página siguiente)
フェルンバンク・サイエンス・センター（科学センター）のレーザー・ショー（次ページに続く）

Atlantans soar to stunning heights...   ...in more ways than one.

Les habitants d'Atlanta s'élèvent vers d'étonnantes hauteurs...   ...de bien des façons.
Atlantaner streben zum Höchsten...   ...in mehr als einer Art.
Los habitantes de Atlanta se elevan a alturas impresionantes...   ...en más de un sentido.
宙に舞い上がるアトランタの人々・・・   ・・・やり方も各人各様。

The two tallest: Georgia-Pacific Building (left), 52 floors high; and Peachtree Plaza Hotel, world's tallest hotel, 72 floors.

Les 2 plus hautes immeubles: Georgia-Pacific (à gauche) avec ses 52 étages, et le Peachtree Plaza Hotel, le plus haute hôtel du monde avec ses 72 étages.

Die zwei höchsten Gebäuder: Georgia-Pacific (links), 52 Stockwerke hoch; und Peachtree Plaza Hotel, das höchste Hotel der Welt, 72 Stockwerke.

Los dos más altos edificios: Georgia-Pacific (izq.), 52 pisos; y el Peachtree Plaza Hotel, el más alto del mundo, 72 pisos.

二大高層ビル：ジョージア・パシフィック・ビル（左、52階建て）と、世界一高いホテルで知られる
ピーチツリー・プラザ・ホテル（72階建て）。

The world is invited: live with Atlanta...

Le monde entier est invité à vivre au rythme d'Atlanta...
Die Welt ist eingeladen mit Atlanta zu leben...
Todo el mundo está invitado: viva con Atlanta...
どなたも歓迎：アトランタと共に暮そう・・・

. . . à y étudier . . .
. . . mit Atlanta zu lernen . . .
. . . estudie en Atlanta . . .
・・・アトランタと共に学ぼう・・・

Agnes Scott College
Le collège supérieur d'Agnes Scott
Agnes Scott College
Colegio universitario Agnes Scott
アグネス・スコット大学

Georgia State University
L'Université de Georgia State
Georgia Staatsuniversität
Universidad Georgia State
ジョージア州立大学

Atlanta University
L'Université d'Atlanta
Atlanta Universität
Universidad Atlanta
アトランタ大学

Emory University
Emory University
Emory Universität
Emory University
エモリー大学

...luxuriate with Atlanta.

...à se réjouir avec Atlanta.
...mit Atlanta in Luxus zu schwelgen.
...disfrute de Atlanta.
・・・アトランタと共に楽しもう。

Hyatt Regency Hotel
L'Hôtel Hyatt Regency
Hyatt Regency Hotel
Hotel Hyatt Regency
ハイアット・リージェンシー・ホテル

Omni International Hotel
L'Hôtel Omni International
Omni Internationales Hotel
Hotel Omni International
オムニ国際ホテル

At right: Peachtree Plaza Hotel
À droite: Le Peachtree Plaza Hotel
Rechts: Peachtree Plaza Hotel
A la derecha: Peachtree Plaza Hotel
右：ピーチツリー・プラザ・ホテル

From government...

Du gouvernement...
Von der Regierung...
Tanto el Gobierno...
政府や・・・

State Capitol dome
Le dôme du Capitol
Kuppel des Regierungsgebäudes
Cúpula del Capitolio
州会議事堂ドーム

...and the leaders...

...et les hommes politiques...
...und die Führern...
...y el integrantes...
•••指導者から•••

State Capitol grounds
Les jardins du Capitol
Anlagen des Regierungsgebäudes
Los jardines del Capitolio
州会議事堂構内

Governor's Mansion
La résidence du Gouverneur
Wohnsitz des Gouverneurs
Residencia del Gobernador
州知事邸宅

Mayor Andrew Young
Andrew Young, le maire d'Atlanta
Bürgermeister Andrew Young
Andrew Young, alcalde de Atlanta
アンドルー・ヤング市長

. . . to the people . . .

. . . aux habitants . . .
. . . zu der Bevöklerung . . .
. . . como así también sus habitantes . . .
・・・一般市民にいたるまで・・・

. . .from big business. . .

...des entreprises de grande envergure...
...vom "big business"...
...las grandes firmas...
・・・大企業から・・・

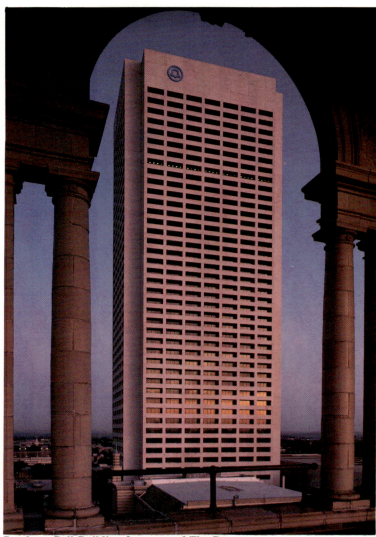

Southern Bell Building from top of The Ponce condominiums
L'immeuble de Southern Bell vu du dernier étage de la résidence Le Ponce
Southern Bell Bau, gesehen vom höchsten Punkt der Ponce condominiums
Vista del edificio Southern Bell desde los condominio Ponce
ポンセ・ド・レオン・アパートの屋上から見たサザン・ベルのビル

The Coca-Cola Company's headquarters tower
La tour de la compagnie Coca-Cola où se trouve le siège de la société
Turm des Hauptsitzes der Coca-Cola Kompanie
Oficinas de la sede central de Coca-Cola Company
コカコーラ社本部タワー

Technology exhibit: Georgia World Congress Center

Le salon de la technologie: une exposition au Georgia World Congress Center
Technologische Ausstellung: Georgia Welt Congress-Zentrum
Exposición Tecnológica en el Georgia World Congress Center
ジョージア・ワールド・コングレス・センターの技術展示場

Airplane tail assembly at Lockheed-Marietta Company

L'assemblage de l'empennage d'un avion à la Société Lockheed-Marietta
Flugzeugmontage in der Lockheed Marietta Kompanie
Montaje de la cola de avión de la compañía Lockheed-Marietta
ロッキード・ジョージア社の航空機尾翼

**Next page: Partners in the sky . . . a Scientific-Atlanta
satellite dish and the moon**

Page suivante: Compagnons de l'espace . . . un satellite de Scientific-Atlanta et la lune
Nächste Seite: Partner am Himmel . . . Scientific-Atlanta Satellite schüssel und
der Mond
Página siguiente: Compañeros en el espacio . . . un satélite Scientific-Atlanta y la luna
次ページ: 空のパートナー…
サイエンティフィック・アトランタの衛星アンテナと月

...to the workers...

...aux travailleurs...
...zu den Arbeitern...
...los trabajadores...
・・・勤労者にいたるまで・・・

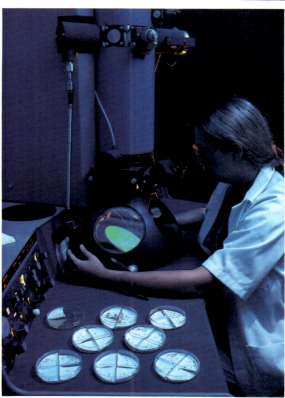

...from cultural attractions...

...des évènements culturels...

...von kulturellen Attraktionen...

...sus atracciones culturales...

・・・文化的催し物から・・・

Concert: Chastain Park
Un concert à Chastain Park
Konzert: Chastain Park
Concierto en Chastain Park
コンサート：チャスティーン・パーク

Interior: Fox Theatre
L'intérieur du Fox Theatre
Innenausstattung: Fox Theater
Interior del Fox Theatre
インテリア：フォックス劇場

High Museum of Art
Le Musée High
High Kunstmuseum
El Museo High (Bellas Artes)
ハイ・ミュージアム・オブ・アート（美術館）

Sculpture on Spring Street
Sculpture sur rue Spring
Skulptur an der Springstrasse
Escultura en Calle Spring
ピーチツリーの彫刻

. . .to the crafts people. . .

...aux artisans d'art...
...zu den Kunstgewerblern...
...obra artesanal...
・・・技芸家にいたるまで・・・

...from the energetic city...

...de la ville trépidante...
...von der lebhaften Stadt...
...desde la pujante ciudad...
・・・活気にあふれた街角から・・・

Renaissance Park: condominiums near downtown
Rennaissance Park: Une résidence près du centre de la ville
Renaissance Park: Condominiums Nähe der Stadtmitte
Renaissance Park: Condominio habitacional cerca del centro de la ciudad
ルネッサンス・スクエア: ダウンタウンに近いアパート

Next page: The business center, downtown
Page suivante: Le quartier des affaires dans le Centre-ville
Nächste Seite: Des Geschäftszentrum in der Stadtmitte
Página siguiente: La zona comercial del centro de la ciudad
次ページ: ダウンタウンのビジネス・センター

Flatiron Building
Equitable Building
Candler Building
Georgia-Pacific Building
55 Park Place

...to the restful countryside...

...à la campagne reposante...
...zu der ruhevollen Umgebung...
...hasta la apacible vida de campo...
・・・心休まる田園地帯にいたるまで・・・

...dining in...

...du dîner à la maison...
...zu Hause zu essen...
...cenando en casa...
・・・家庭でのもてなしに・・・

Dailey's Restaurant & Bar
デイリーズ・レストランとバー

International Food Works restaurant
Le restaurant "International Food Works"
"International Food Works" restaurant
Restaurante "International Food Works"
インターナショナル・フード・ワークス・レストラン

. . . or dining out . . .

. . . au dîner à l'extérieur. . .
. . . oder auswärts. . .
. . . o fuera. . .
・・・また、外での食事に・・・

. . .from the peace of sacred halls. . .

. . .de la quiétude des lieux saints. . .
. . .von Frieden der heiligen Hallen. . .
. . .desde la paz de los templos sagrados. . .
・・・聖堂の静けさから・・・

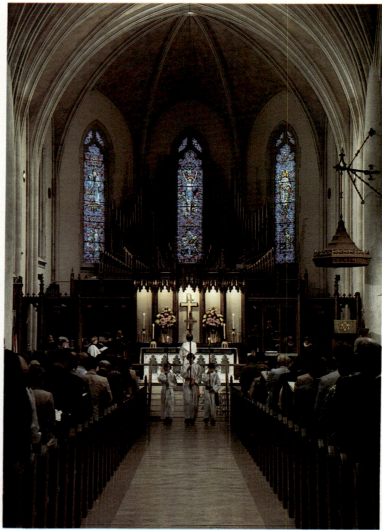

Ebenezer Baptist Church
Le temple baptiste "Ebenezer"
Ebenezer Baptisten Kirche
Iglesia Bautista "Ebenezer"
エベネーザー・バプティスト教会

Episcopal Cathedral of St. Philip
La cathédrale de St. Philip
Episcopalkathedtrale St. Philip
Catedral Episcopal de St. Philip
セイント・フィリップ聖公会

The Temple synagogue
La synagogue "The Temple"
Die Temple Synagogo
Singago "The Temple"
ユダヤ教会堂

Episcopal Cathedral of St. Philip
La cathédrale de St. Philip
Episcopalkathedrale St. Philip
Catedral Episcopal de St. Philip
セイント・フィリップ聖公会

...to the tumult of big league sports...

...au tumulte des grands évènements sportifs...
...zum Tumult der Nationalsporte...
...hasta el bullicio de los grandes eventos deportivos...
・・・にぎやかな全国リーグ・スポーツ大会にいたるまで・・・

The Atlanta Falcons
Les Falcons: l'équipe de football d'Atlanta
Die Atlanta Falcons
Los Atlanta Falcons
アトランタ・ファルコンズ（フットボールチーム）

The Atlanta Braves
Les Braves: l'équipe de baseball d'Atlanta
Die Atanta Braves
Los Atlanta Braves
アトランタ・ブレーブズ（野球チーム）

Next page: New angle on The Atlanta Hawks in Omni Coliseum
Page suivante: un regard différent sur les Hawks, l'équipe de basketball d'Atlanta à l'Omni Coliseum
Nächste Seite: Neue Perspektive der Atlanta Hawks in Omni Kolosseum
La siguiente página:
Los Atlanta Hawks vistos desde un angulo diferente en el Omni Coliseum
次ページ: 新しいアングルを見せるオムニ大競技場の
アトランタ・ホークス

...Atlanta is for everyone.

...Atlanta plaît à tout le monde.
...Atlanta ist für Jeden.
...Atlanta es para todos nosotros.
・・・誰もが楽しめる町、それがアトランタだ。

Mayor Andrew Young makes a friend
Le maire Andrew Young fait un ami
Bürgermeister Andrew Young macht Freunde
El alcalde Andrew Young, fraternizando
アンドルー・ヤング市長と友達に

Relaxing in Hurt Park
Détente à Hurt Park
Erholung im "Hurt Park"
Descansando en el Parque Hurt
ハート・パークでのんびり……

By the light of fresh day...

En suivant la lumière d'un jour nouveau...
Im Licht des neuen Tages...
A la luz de un nuevo día...
あけぼのの光と・・・

. . . or the glisten of night . . .

. . . ou la splendeur de la nuit . . .
. . . oder beim Gefunkel der Nacht . . .
. . . o del esplendor de la noche . . .
・・・夜のきらめきに導かれて・・・

. . . in summer or winter . . .

. . .en été comme en hiver. . .
. . .im Sommer oder Winter. . .
. . .en verano o invierno. . .
・・・夏も冬も変らずに・・・

. . .und Tower Place, glitzert im Winter

Colony Square basking in summer. . .
Colony Square ensoleillé en été. . .
Colony Square sonnt sich em Sommer. . .
Colony Square bajo el sol del verano. . .
夏の日ざしを浴びるコロニー・スクエア…

. . .and Tower Place, glistening in winter
. . .et Tower Place, resplendissant en hiver
. . .und Tower Place, glitzert im Winter
. . .y Tower Place, resplandeciente en invierno
…冬の日ざしに輝くタワー・プレイス

...all ways lead to Atlanta.

...tous les chemins mènent à Atlanta.
...alle Strassen führen nach Atlanta.
...todos los caminos conducen a Atlanta.
・・・いずこの途もアトランタに通じる。

Hartsfield Atlanta International Airport
Hartsfield, L'aéroport international d'Atlanta
Hartsfield Atlanta, Internationaler Flughafen
Hartsfield, el aeropuerto internacional de Atlanta
ハートフィールド・アトランタ国際空港

Interlocking freeways...and rails for freight
Les autoroutes se croisant...et des rails pour le frêt
Ineinandergreifende Autobahnen...und Frachtlinien
Autopistas entrelazadas...y ferrocarriles de carga
高速道路網と貨物運送用鉄道

It takes pride in its defenders...

Elle est fière de ses défenseurs...
Sie rühmt sich ihrer Beschützer...
Orgullosa de quienes la defienden...
プライド高き防衛陣・・・

Dobbins Air Force Base
Dobbins, une base de l'armée de l'air
Dobbins Luftwaffe Stützpunkt
Dobbins, base de la Fuerza Aérea
ドビンズ空軍基地

. . . and its patriots.

...et de ses patriotes.
...und ihrer Patrioten.
...y de sus patriotas.
・・・プライド高き小さな愛国者。

It is a city of whimsey...

C'est une ville extravagante...
Sie ist eine Stadt mit Stimmung...
Es una ciudad extravagante...
奇抜なアイデアが生まれる町・・・

The Toy Museum
Le Musée du jouet
Das Spielzeugmuseum
El Museo de Juguett
玩具博物館

. . . and high technology . . .

. . . à la haute technologie . . .
. . . und hoher Technik . . .
. . . de alta tecnología . . .
・・・ハイテクノロジーの町・・・

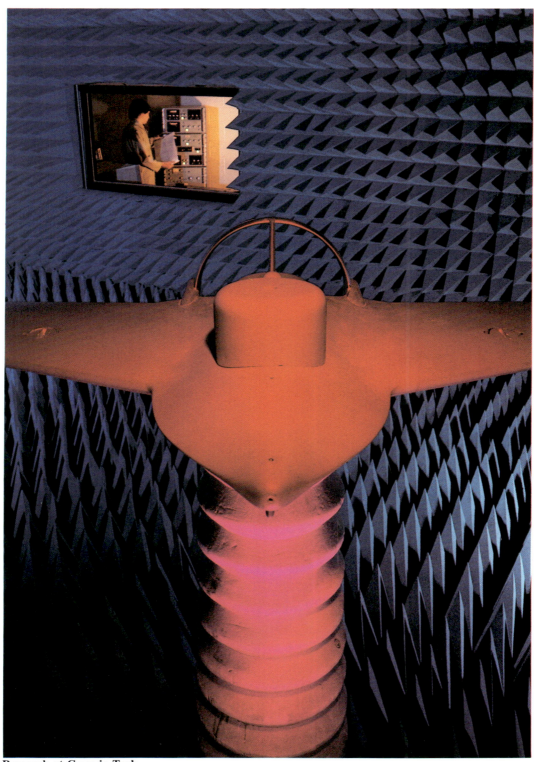

Research at Georgia Tech
La recherche à Georgia Tech
Forschung an Georgia Tech
Investigando en Georgia Tech
ジョージア・テクでの研究活動

...the largest airport in the world...

...le plus grand aéroport du monde...
...mit dem grössten Flughafen der Welt...
...el aeropuerto más grande del mundo...
・・・世界一の空港のある町・・・

...and elegant homes...

...des demeures élégantes...

...eleganten Häusern...

...y elegantes viviendas...

•••エレガントな住宅と•••

...with extraordinary interiors.

...avec des intérieurs extraordinaires.
...mit aussergewöhnlichen Einrichtungen.
...con maravillosos interiores.
・・・豪華な室内装飾が生まれた町。

Stylish kitchen for stylish cooking...
Une cuisine élégante pour la préparation de plats raffinés...
Flotte Küche für flottes Essen...
Elegante cocina para cocinar con estilo...
料理はスタイルを生かして…モダンなキッチン

...and a den for relaxing
...et un coin pour se détendre
...und ein Familienzimmer zum Ausruhen
...y un rincón para descanso y esparcimiento
…茶室でリラックス

The night life beckons...

Le vie nocturne captive...
Das Nachtleben lockt...
Le vida nocturna se manifiesta...
ナイトライフへの招待・・・

Cocktails at the plush Atlanta Hilton Hotel
L'heure de l'apéritif dans le luxueux Hôtel Atlanta Hilton
Cocktails in dem prunkvollen Atlanta Hilton Hotel
Cócteles y aperitivos en el lujoso Hotel Atlanta Hilton
豪華なアトランタ・ヒルトン・ホテルでカクテルを・・・

A play in Gene & Gabe's Upstairs
Une pièce de théâtre à Gene & Gabe's Upstairs
Eine Aufführung im "Gene & Gabe's Upstairs" Theater
Presentando una obra en el "Gene & Gabe's Upstairs"
ジーン・アンド・ゲイブス・アップステアーズにて演じられる劇

Coach and Six: Celebrity mural behind the bar
La fresque avec ses célébrités derritère le bar du restaurant Coach and Six
Coach and Six Restaurant: Hinter der Bar Wandgemälde berühmter Personen
El restaurante Coach and Six y su Mural de Celebridades en el bar
コーチ・アンド・シックス: バーの後にかかった名士の壁画

...and sports play without end.

...et les sports se jouent sans fin.

...und Sportvorführungen gehen an, ohne Ende.

...y los deportes se suceden sin interrupción.

・・・尽きることのないスポーツ。

Atlanta World of Tennis professional tournament
Le tournoi de tennis professionnel "Atlanta World of Tennis"
Professionelles Tennis Tournament im Atlanta World of Tennis
Torneo profesional en el "Atlanta World of Tennis"
アトランタのテニス・プロ・トーナメント

The Atlanta Steeplechase
Le Steeple-chase d'Atlanta
Das Atlanta Hindernissrennen
Concurso Hípico de Atlanta
アトランタの障害物競争

Next page: The Atlanta Golf Classic
Page suivante: Le tournoi de golf "Atlanta Golf Classic"
Nächste Seite: Die Atlanta Golf-Klassik
Página siguiente: el Clásico de golf en Atlanta
次ページ：アトランタ・ゴルフ・トーナメント

Here are the best in medicine...

On y trouve une médecine à la pointe du progrès...
Hier sind die Besten im medizinischen Gebiet...
Aquí se encuentra lo más avanzado en médicina...
医療で・・・

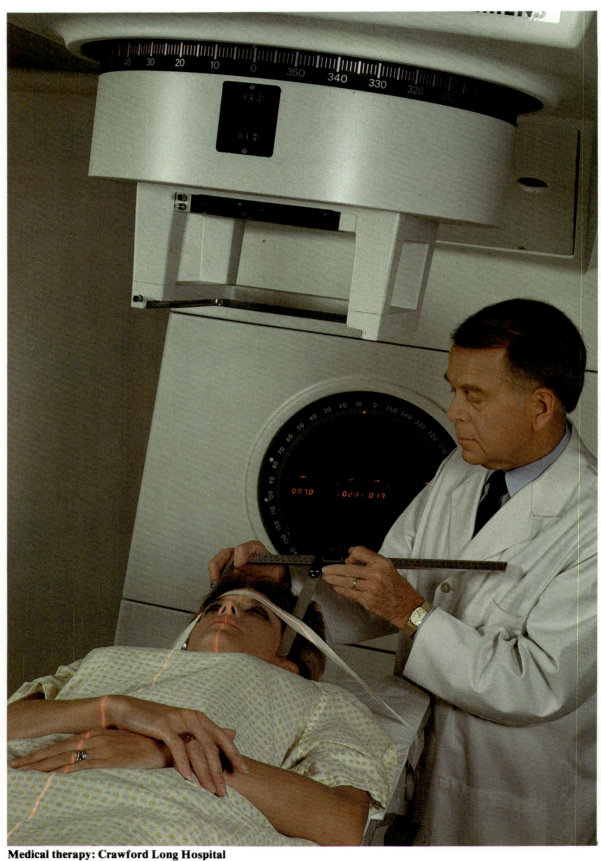

Medical therapy: Crawford Long Hospital
Thérapeutique à l'hôspitál Crawford Long
Medizinischer Behandlung: Crawford Long Hospital
Terapia medical en el hospital Crawford Long
医療: クローフォード・ロング病院

. . .and the media. . .

. . .des moyens de communications ultra-modernes. . .
. . .und in der Media. . .
. . .y en commicaciones. . .
・・・マスコミで・・・

Turner Broadcasting System: a giant in cable
Turner Broadcasting System: un studio de télévision géant
Turners Rundfunksystem: Ein Riese der Kabeln
Turner Broadcasting System: un gigante de cable-TV
ターナー放送システム: 巨大なケーブル

. . .spectacular new structures. . .

...des structures d'avant-garde...

...grossartige neue Bauten...

...nuevas estructuras que son espectaculares...

•••壮観な新建造物で•••

Buildings house the Standard Federal Savings & Loan Assn. (left) and the First National Bank (center)

Les immeubles qui abritent la Standard Federal Savings & Loan Assn. (à gauche) et la First National Bank (centre)

Gebäude, die die Standard Federal Savings & Loan Assn. (links) und die First Nationalbank (mtte) behaust

Edificios que albergan la Standard Federal Savings & Loan Assn. (izq.) y el First National Bank

当ビルには、スタンダード・フェデラル・セイビングズ・

アンド・ローン・アソシエーション（貯蓄貸付組合；左）と

ファースト・ナショナル・バンク（銀行；中央）が

入っている。

. . .and dignified edifices.

. . .et des demeures classiques.

. . .und stattliche Gebäude.

. . .y elegantes moradas de estilo clásico.

・・・おごそかな大邸宅で、ここは一番。

Swan House: part of Atlanta Historical Society
Swan House: une partie de l'Atlanta Historical Society
Swan Hause: teil der Atlanta historischen Gesellschaft
Swan House: parte de la Atlanta Historical Society
スワン・ハウス：アトランタ史学協会

Next page: Swan House interior
Page suivante: l'intérieur de lSwan House
Nächste Seite: innenausstattug des Swan Hauses
Página siguiente: interior de l residencia Swan House
次ページ：スワン・ハウス内

Atlanta has it all . . .

Atlanta a d'infinies richesses...
Atlanta hat alles...
Atlanta lo tiene todo...
アトランタにはすべてがある・・・

Piedmont Arts Festival
Le Festival des Arts à Piedmont Park
Piedmont Kunstfestlichkeiten
Festival Artístico Piedmont
ピードモント芸術祭

A band of smiling faces . . . and happy feet
Un groupe de visages souriants . . . et des pieds dansants
Eine Schar von lachenden Gesichtern . . . und fröhlicher Füsse
Un grupo de caras sonrientes . . . y pies alegres
笑みをうかべて……足も軽やかに……ブラスバンド

. . . gardens of serenity . . .

. . . des jardins pleins de sérénité . . .
. . . ruhespendende Gärten . . .
. . . jardines apacibles . . .
・・・静閑な庭園・・・

Atlanta Botanical Gardens (above); Midtown (below); Fernbank Science Center (right)
Les jardins botaniques d'Atlanta (ci-dessus); au centre de la ville (ci-dessous); Le centre scientifique de Fernbank (à droite)
Atlantas Botanischer Garten (oben); in der Stadtmitte (unten) Fernbank wissenschaftliches Zentrum (rechts)
Jardines Botánicos de Atlanta (arriba); del centro de la ciudad (debajo); Centro Científico Fernbank (derecha)
アトランタ植物園（上）、ウィン・パーク（下）、フェルンバンク・サイエンス・センター（科学センター；右）

...churches to soothe the soul...

...des églises pour la paix de l'âme...
...Kirchen, die die Seele erleichtern...
...iglesias para solaz del alma...
・・・心の落ちつく教会・・・

Second Ponce de Leon Baptist Church
Le temple baptiste "Second Ponce de Leon"
Zweite Ponce de Leon Baptisten Kirche
Segunda Iglesia Bautista "Ponce de León"
第二ポンセ・ド・レオン・バプティスト教会

Greek Orthodox Cathedral of the Annunciation
L'église orthodoxe grecque de l'Annonciation
Griechich orthodox Kathedrale der Verkündigung
Catedral de la Anunciación de la Iglesia Griega Ortodoxa
ギリシャ告知正教会
（ギリシャ・オーソドックス・キャシードラル・オブ・ザ・アナンシエーション）

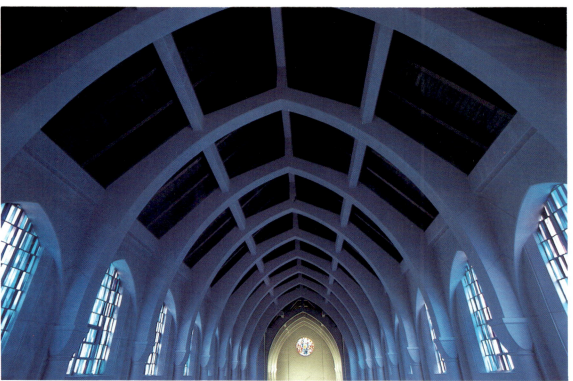

Monastery of the Holy Ghost (Conyers)
Le monastère du Saint Esprit (Conyers)
Kloster des Heiligen Geistes (Conyers)
Monasterio del Espíritu Santo (Conyers)
聖霊の修道院（コニヤズ）

. . .and organized sports to rouse the spirit.

. . .et des compétitions sportives pour stimuler l'espirit.

. . .und organisierter Sport, um den Geist anzuregen.

. . .y una estimulante variedad de deportes.

・・・そして心浮きたつスポーツ大会。

Above, Commerce Dragstrip; at right, Road Atlanta Raceway
Ci-dessus, Commerce Dragstrip; à droite, le "Road Atlanta Raceway"
Oben, Commerce Dragstrip; rechts, "Road Atlanta Raceway"
Arriba, Commerce Dragstrip; a la derecha, "Road Atlanta Raceway"
上と右: アトランタ・ロードのレース場

Next page: Atlanta Stadium, site of major sports and other events

Page suivante: Le Stade d'Atlanta, l'endroit où ont lieu les plus grands évènements sportifs

Nächste Seite: Atlanta Stadium, Platz für grosse Sportveranstaltungen und andere Ereignisse

Página siguiente: Atlanta Stadium, el escenario de los más importantes encuentros deportivos y otros eventos de magnitud

次ページ：スポーツ・催し物の会場となるアトランタ・スタジアム

The city, ever in motion...

Le ville, en perpéturel mouvement...
Die Stadt, immer in Bewegung...
La ciudad, siempre dinámica...
活気ある町・・・

Six Flags thrill ride
Le grand frisson: un tour de montagnes russes à Six Flags
Six Flags Schauerfahrt
Un paseo estremecedor en Six Flags
シックス・フラッグの乗り物はスリル満点

Sailing on Lake Lanier
Un jour de voile sur le lac Lanier
Segeln auf dem Lanier See
Veleros en el lago Lanier
ラニア湖でヨット遊び

. . . is a haven for the young . . .

. . .engageante pour les jeunes. . .
. . .ist eine Zuflucht für die Jugend. . .
. . .un imán para los jóvenes. . .
・・・若者の天国・・・

. . .and quiet harbor for the elderly.

. . .accueillante pour les plus âgés.
. . .und ein ruhiger Hafen für die Betagten.
. . .y un refugio para la gente mayor.
・・・老人達の憩の場がある静かな波止場。

Whether you look up at Atlanta...

Que vous regardiez Atlanta d'en bas...
Ob Sie Atlanta von oben sehen...
Aunque usted contemple a Atlanta desde abajo...
アトランタは上を向いても・・・

Georgia Power Co. headquarters, with field of units to harness the sun's power
Le siége de la Compagnie Georgia Power avec un champ d'éléments photo-sensibles pour capter l'énergie solaire
Georgia Elektrizitätswek, Hauptsitz, mit Einrichtungen, um die Sonnenkraft nutzbar zu machen
Sede central de Georgia Power Company con una red de unidades para aprovechamiento de la energia solar
ジョージア電力会社本部、太陽エネルギーを利用した発電施設

Atlanta Civic Center
Le Centre Civique d'Atlanta
Atlanta Volkszentrum
Centro Cívico de Atlanta
アトランタ中央官庁区

...whether you see it up close...

...de près...
...ob sie von der Nähe sehen...
...de cerca...
・・・近づいて見ても・・・

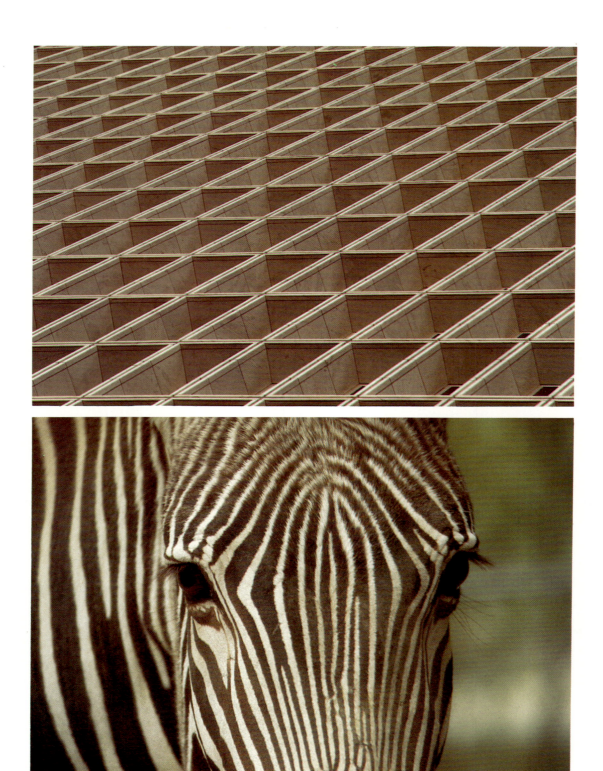

At Grant Park Zoo
Le jardin zoologique de Grant Park
Im Grantpark Zoo
Jardin zoológico en Grant Park
グラント・パーク動物園にて

Taking a leaf from Nature
Une feuille de la nature
Ein Blatt aus der Natur nehmend
Tomando una hoja de la Naturaleza
自然に習って…

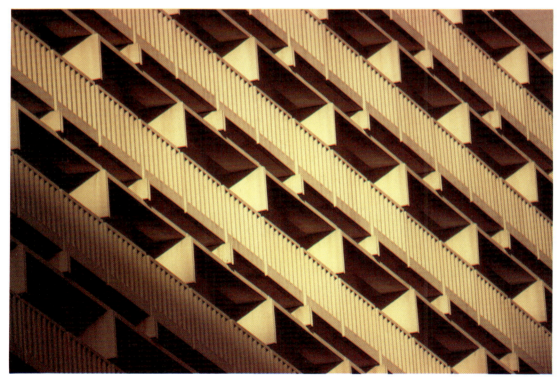

. . . or from far away . . .

...ou de loin...
...oder der Ferne...
...o de le jos...
・・・遠くから見ても・・・

Stone Mountain
ストーン山

Inside Atlanta Library's main branch
A l'intérieur de la bibliothèque d'Atlanta
Im Hauptzweig der Atlanta Bibliothek
Interior de la sede central de la biblioteca de Atlanta
アトランタ図書本部館内

. . .ou en descendant. . .
. . .oder herunter kommen. . .
. . .o bajando. . .
・・・降りても・・・

Into the heart of the Georgia World Congress Center
Un regard vers le Georgia World Congress Center
Hinein in das Herz des Georgia Welt Kongress-Zentrums
Hacia el interior del Georgia World Congress Center
ジョージア・ワールド・コングレス・センターの中央部

...you cannot miss the city's beauty...

...la beauté de la ville ne peut vous échapper...
...Sie können die Schönheit der Stadt nicht übersehen...
...Ud. se encontrará permanentemente inmerso en su belleza...
・・・市の美しさは変ることなく・・・

Vinings Inn
L'auberge Vinings Inn
Vinings Gasthof
La hostería Vinings Inn
ビニングス・イン

...and its ever-changing variety.

...ni sa jeunesse sans cesse renouvelée.
...und ihre dauernde Veränderung.
...y en su continua variedad.

・・・その多様性は尽きることがない。

A rare snow imprisons cars at the Airport
Une neige inhabituelle immoblise les viotures à l'aéroport
Seltener Schneefall hält Auto am Flughafen fest
Una nevada inusual inmobiliza automóviles en el aeropuerto
めずらしい大雪で動きがとれなくなった車輌、空港駐車場にて。

Atlanta is proud of its striking structures...

Atlanta est fière de son architecture remarquable...
Atlanta ist stolz auf ihre eindrucksvollen Bauten...
Atlanta está orgullosa de sus imponentes estructuras...
アトランタが誇る立派な建造物・・・

Tower Place
タワー・プレイス

◀Peachtree Plaza Hotel pool
La piscine de l'hotel Peachtree Plaza
Schwimmbad des Peachtree Plaza Hotels
La piscina del Hotel Peachtree Plaza
ピーチツリー・プラザ・ホテルのプール

Next page: Lobby of the Waverly Hotel
Page suivante: Le hall de l'hôtel Waverly
Nächste Seite: Vorhalle des Waverly Hotels
Página siguiente: Recepción del hotel Waverly
次ページ：ウェーバリー・ホテルのロビー

. . . its warm people . . .

. . . ses habitants chaleureux . . .
. . . ihre warmherzigen Leute . . .
. . . su gente cordial . . .
・・・暖かい人々・・・

. . .its sculptured art . . .

. . .son art sculptural. . .
. . .ihre bildhauerische Kunst. . .
. . .su arte escultórico. . .
・・・彫刻芸術・・・

Eagle at Federal Reserve Building
L'Aigle de l'immeuble Federal Reserve
Adler am Bundesmünzamt
Aguila frente al edificio Federal Reserve
連邦準備銀行ビルのワシ

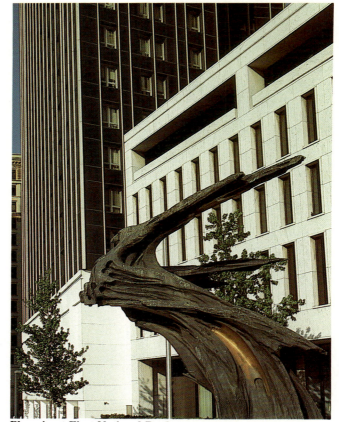

Phoenix at First National Bank
Le phoenix de First National Bank
Phönix an der First Nationalbank
Fénix en el First National Bank
ファースト・ナショナル・バンクのフェニックス（不死鳥）

At the Equitable Building
Dans l'immeuble Equitable
Das Equitable-Gebäude
En el edificio Equitable
エクィタブル・ビルで……

Robert W. Woodruff Arts Center

Next page: Sculpture at Peachtree Center
Page suivante: Une sculpture à Peachtree Center
Nächste Seite: Skulpture im Peachtree Center
La siguiente página: Escultura en el Peachtree Center
次ページ: ピーチツリー・センターの彫像

...its artful buildings...

...ses immeubles ingénieux...
...ihre kunstvollen Bauten...
...sus ingeniosos edificios...
・・・凝った建築物・・・.

Omni Coliseum
L'Omni Coliseum
Omni Kolosseum
Omni Coliseum
オムニ大競技場

Firemen's Fund Building
L'immeuble de Fireman's Fund
"Fireman's Fund" Gebäude
Edificio "Fireman's Fund"
ファイアーマンズ・ファンド・ビル

...inside...and out.

...à l'intérieur...et à l'extérieur.

...innen...und aussen.

...tanto por dentro...como por fuera.

・・・それは、表も・・・裏も変りない。

Healey Building lobby
Le hall de l'immeuble Healey
Vorhalle im Healey Gebäude
Recepción del edificio Healey
ヒーリー・ビルのロビー

The Ponce foyer
L'entrée de la residence Ponce
Ponce Foyer
Hall de entrada de los apartementos ponce
ポンセ・ド・レオン・アパートの玄関

Summit Building
L'immeuble Summit
Summitgebäude
Edificio Summit
サミット・ビル

Atlanta welcomes industry...

Atlanta ouvre grand ses portes à l'industrie...
Atlanta begrüsst Industrie...
Atlanta se complace en acoger las industrias...
アトランタは産業を奨励し・・・

Georgia Power Company's Plant Bowen: coal fired generators
L'usine Bowen de la société Georgia Power: des génératrices alimentées au charbon
Werk Bowen der Georgia Power Company: Generatoren betieben mit Kohle
Planta Bowen de Georgia Power: generadores por combustion de carbón
ジョージア電力会社のボーウェン工場: 石炭発電機

...and the industrious.

...et aux personnes industrieuses.

...und die Fleissigen.

...y las gentes laboriosas.

・・・勤勉を尊ぶ。

Working on railroad wheels

En train de travailler sur des roues de chemin de fer

Arbeit auf Eisenbahnrädern

Trabajando en las ruedas de un tren

電車の中で……

Working on a generator at Plant Bowen

L'entretien d'une génératrice à l'usine Bowen

Arbeiten am Generator im Werk Bowen

Trabajando en un generador en la Planta Bowen

ボーウェン工場発電機: 作業中風景

It prizes modern luxury . . .

Elle apprécie le luxe moderne...
Sie schätzt modernen Luxus...
Valora el lujo moderno...
ここでは、近代的贅沢と・・・

. . . and touches of the past.

. . . et les charmes du passé.
. . . und Spuren der Vergangenheit.
. . . y los toques de antigüedad.

• • •唯緒ある歴史が共存する。

Coca-Cola memorabilia
Des souvenirs de Coca-Cola
Coca-Cola Denkwürdigkeiten
Souvenirs Coca-Cola
コカコーラ社の言行録

Antique show (Red Baron)
Le salon des antiquaires (Red Baron)
Antiquitätenausstellung (Red Baron)
Salón de antigüedades (Red Baron)
骨董品展示会

It's a city of gracious people...

C'est une ville pleine de gens aimables...
Sie ist eine Stadt zuvorkommender Leute...
Es una ciudad rebosante de gente amable...
優しい人々のいる町・・・

...and graceful homes...

...et de demeures élégantes...
...und geschmackvoller Häuser...
...y elegantes viviendas...
・・・シックな家並のある町・・・

. . . brilliant technicians . . .

...de techniciens brillants...
...hervorragender Techniker...
...técnicos brillantes, ingeniosos...
・・・優れた技術者に恵まれた町・・・

Western Electric Co.
La société Western Electric
Western Elektrizitäts Co.
Compañía Western Electric
ウェスタン・エレクトリック社

. . . and visionary technology.

. . .et d'une technologie innovatrice.
. . .und zukunftsreicher Technologie.
. . .y tecnología visionaria.
・・・そして未来の技術が開ける町。

Maintenance on airplane jet engine
Entretien de moteurs d'avions à réaction
Reparation des Flugzeug Jets
Mantenimiento de turbinas de avión
航空機ジェット・エンジンの保守

Next page: American Telephone and Telegraph Company Long Lines Operations Center
Page suivante: Le centre des opérations de communications à longue distance de la société American Telephone and Telegraph Company
Nächste Seite: Ferngesprächs Zentrale der American Telephone and Telegraph Company.
La siguiente página: Centro de operaciones para larga distancia de la compañia American Telephone and Telegraph
次ページ: アメリカ電話電信会社 長距離線運営センター

TO THE
ATLANTA REGIONAL
ETWORK MANAGEMENT CENTER
INTRA-REGIONAL NETWORK
ATL

The world of Atlanta is for everyone...

L'univers d'Atlanta est pour tout le monde...
Atlantas Welt ist für Alle...
El mundo de Atlanta es para todos...
アトランタの世界はみんなのもの・・・

Peachtree Center
ピーチツリー・センター

. . . and everything.

. . .et pour tout.
. . .und Alles.
. . .y para todo.
・・・そしてここにはすべてがある。

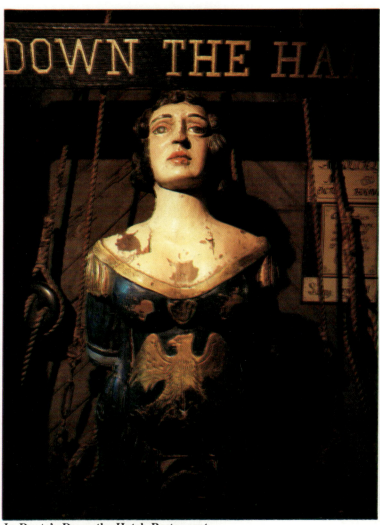

In Dante's Down the Hatch Restaurant
Au restaurant Dante's Down the Hatch
Im Dantes Down the Hatch Restaurant
Restaurante Dante's Down the Hatch
ダンテズ・ダウン・ザ・ハッチ・レストラン

Wedding outdoors at The Mansion, a restaurant
Un mariage en plein air au restaurant The Mansion
Hochzeit im Freien vor der Mansion, ein Restaurant
Casamiento al aire libre en el restaurante The Mansion
レストラン・マンションでの屋外結婚式

The city is alive with construction...

La ville foisonne de constructions...
Die Stadt ist rege mit Konstruktion...
La ciudad bulle; con la construcción...
活気づく町アトランタ。建設工事に・・・

. . . production . . .

. . . de productions . . .
. . . Produktion . . .
. . . producción . . .
・・・生産に・・・

Georgia Power Company operations center
Centre de commandes de la société Georgia Power
Kontrollcenter der Georgia Power Company
Centro de controles de Georgia Power Company
ジョージア電力会社運営センター

At Atlantic Steel Co.
La société Atlantic Steel Co.
Die Gesellschaft "Atlantic Steel Co."
En la compañia Atlantic Steel
アトランティック・スチール社にて

...preservation...

...de conservations...
...Konservation...
...conservación...
・・・保存・保護に・・・

Rhodes-Haverty Building
L'immeuble de Rhodes-Haverty
Rhodes-Haverty Bau
El edificio Rhodes-Haverty
ローデス・ハバティー・ビル

. . .and illumination. . .

. . .et d'illuminations. . .
. . .und Illumination. . .
. . .e iluminación. . .
・・・そして、イルミネーションに・・・

Dome on the Hyatt Regency Hotel
Le dôme de l'hôtel Hyatt Regency
Kuppel des Hyatt Regency Hotel
Cúpula del hotel Hyatt Regency
ハイアット・リージャンシー・ホテルのドーム

At left, the "101 Marietta Building"
A gauche, l'immeuble "101 Marietta"
Links, das "101 Marietta Building"
A la izquierda, el edificio "Marietta 101"
左、マリエッタ・ビル101番

. . . contemplation . . .

. . . de contemplations
. . . Betrachtung . . .
. . . contemplación . . .
・・・熟考に・・・

...and association...

...et d'associations...
...und Verbindung...
...y asociación...
・・・そしてグループ形成・討論に・・・

Dining in Colony Square
Díner à Colony Square
Dinieren im Colony Square
Cenando en Colony Square
コロニー・スクエアで食事

...conversation...

...de conversations...

...Unterhaltung...

...conversación...

・・・話し合いに・・・

...recreation...

...de distractions...
...Erholung...
...diversión...
・・・レクリエーションに・・・

. . . and celebration.

. . .et de célébrations.

. . .und Feierlichkeit.

. . .y celebración.

・・・そして祝祭に。

"Light Up Atlanta" celebration, downtown
La fête "Light Up Atlanta," au centre de la ville
"Beleuchte Atlanta" Feierlichkeiten in der Innenstadt
Festival "Light Up Atlanta," en el centro de la ciudad
" アトランタに灯を" の祭典、ダウンタウン